Amelia Kemp

Presented to Jessica Nead

by Aunt Helen, Uncle Brian and Tawnya.

on May 4, 1997.

My First Communion Book

Written by
Daniel J. Porter

Edited by
Rev. Victor Hoagland, C.P.

Illustrated by
Samuel J. Butcher

The Regina Press
New York

Copyright © 1991 Text by The Regina Press
Copyright © 1991 Illustrations by Precious Moments Incorporated
All rights reserved. No part of this book may be reproduced
in any form without permission in writing from the publisher.

Nihil Obstat: Most Rev. Thomas J. Riley, Diocesan Censor Librorum

Imprimatur: + Humberto S. Medeiros, Archbishop of Boston

Date: April 11, 1974

English translation approved by the National Conference of Catholic Bishops and confirmed by the Apostolic See. Published by authority of the Bishops' Committee on the Liturgy.

1991
THE REGINA PRESS
145 Sherwood Avenue
Farmingdale, New York 11735

ISBN: 0-88271-280-2

Printed in Belgium

CONTENTS

INTRODUCTORY RITES

Priest: In the name of the Father, and of the Son, and of the Holy Spirit.

People: Amen.

Greeting

Priest: The grace of our Lord Jesus Christ and the love of God and the fellowship of the Holy Spirit be with you all.

People: And also with you.

(or)

Priest: The grace and peace of God our Father and the Lord Jesus Christ be with you.

People: Blessed be God, the Father of our Lord Jesus Christ.

(or) And also with you.

(or)

Priest: The Lord be with you.

People: And also with you.

Penitential Rite

After the introduction to the day's Mass, the priest invites the people to recall their sins and to repent of them in silence. Then one of the following forms is used.

Priest and people:

I confess to almighty God,
and to you, my brothers and
    sisters,
that I have sinned through my
    own fault
(They strike their breast:)
in my thoughts and in my words,
in what I have done,
and in what I have failed to do;
and I ask blessed Mary, ever
    virgin,
all the angels and saints,
and you, my brothers and sisters,
to pray for me to the Lord our
    God.

(or)

Priest: Lord, we have sinned
against you: Lord, have mercy.

People: Lord have mercy.

Priest: Lord, show us your
mercy and love.

People: And grant us your
salvation.

(or)

Priest (or other minister):

You were sent to heal the contrite:
Lord, have mercy.

People: Lord, have mercy.

Priest (or other minister):

You came to call sinners:
Christ, have mercy.

People: Christ, have mercy.

Priest (or other minister):

You plead for us at the right hand
of the Father:
Lord, have mercy.

People: Lord have mercy.

At the end of each of above forms is said:

Priest: **May almighty God have mercy on us, forgive us our sins, and bring us to everlasting life.**

People: **Amen.**

Kyrie

Unless included in the penitential rite, the Kyrie is sung or said by all, with alternating parts for the choir or cantor and for the people:

V. Lord, have mercy.
R. Lord, have mercy.

V. Christ, have mercy.
R. Christ, have mercy.

V. Lord, have mercy.
R. Lord, have mercy.

Gloria

Glory to God in the highest,
   and peace to his people
   on earth.
Lord God, heavenly King, almighty
God and Father,
   we worship you, we give you
    thanks,
   we praise you for your glory.
Lord Jesus Christ, only Son of
   the Father,
 Lord God, Lamb of God.
 you take away the sin of the
   world:
    have mercy on us;
 you are seated at the right hand
   of the Father:
    receive our prayer.
For you alone are the Holy One,
you alone are the Lord,
you alone are the Most High,

16

Jesus Christ,
with the Holy Spirit,
in the glory of God the Father.
Amen.

Opening Prayer

Priest: Let us pray.

Then the priest says the opening prayer which gives the theme of the day's celebration. He concludes:

Priest: . . . forever and ever.

People: Amen.

LITURGY OF THE WORD

We listen to God's message from Holy Scripture as proclaimed by his prophets and apostles.

First Reading

At the end of the reading:
Reader: **This is the Word of the Lord.**
People: **Thanks be to God.**

Responsorial Psalm

The people repeat the response said by the reader the first time and then after each verse.

Second Reading

At the end of the reading:
Reader: **This is the Word of the Lord.**
People: **Thanks be to God.**

Alleluia

Gospel

Deacon (or Priest): **The Lord be
with you.**

People: **And also with you.**

Deacon (or Priest): **A reading from
the gospel according to
N.**

People: **Glory to you, Lord.**

At the end of the reading:

Deacon (or Priest): **This is the
gospel of the Lord.**

People: **Praise to you, Lord Jesus
Christ.**

Homily

*We have heard God's message, and
now we listen to the words spoken by
the priest about God's message.*

Profession of Faith

We believe in one God,
   the Father, the Almighty,
   maker of heaven and earth,
   of all that is seen and unseen.
We believe in one Lord, Jesus
   Christ,
      the only Son of God,
      eternally begotten of the
         Father,
      God from God, Light from
         Light,
      true God from true God,
      begotten, not made, one in
         Being with the Father.
Through him all things were
      made.
For us men and for our salvation
      he came down from heaven:
by the power of the Holy Spirit

*(All bow at the following words up
to:* and became man.)

he was born of the Virgin
Mary, and became man.
For our sake he was crucified
under Pontius Pilate:
he suffered, died, and was
buried.
On the third day he rose again
in fulfillment of the Scriptures;
he ascended into heaven
and is seated at the right
hand of the Father.
He will come again in glory to
judge the living and the dead,
and his kingdom will have no
end.

We believe in the Holy Spirit,
the Lord, the giver of life,
who proceeds from the Father
and the Son.
With the Father and the Son
he is worshiped and glorified.
He has spoken through the
Prophets.

We believe in one holy catholic
and apostolic Church.
We acknowledge one baptism
for the forgiveness of sins.
We look for the resurrection
of the dead,
and the life of the world to
come. Amen.

General Intercessions
(Prayer of the Faithful)

*We unite with one another to pray for
our needs, for the whole Church and
people everywhere. After the priest
gives the introduction, the deacon or
other minister sings or says the in-
vocations.*

People: **Lord, hear our prayer.**

*(or other response, according to local
customs)*
*At the end the priest says the
concluding prayer:*

People: **Amen.**

LITURGY OF THE EUCHARIST

Offertory Song

We bring bread and wine for the Sacrifice.

Before placing the bread on the altar, the priest says quietly:

Blessed are you, Lord, God of
   all creation.
Through your goodness we have
   this bread to offer,
which earth has given and human
   hands have made.
It will become for us the bread
   of life.

If there is no singing, the people respond:

People: Blessed be God for ever.

Blessed are you, God of
  all creation.
Through your goodness we have
  this wine to offer,
fruit of the vine and work of
  human hands.
It will become our spiritual
  drink.

If there is no singing, the people respond:

People: **Blessed be God for ever.**

Invitation to Prayer

Priest: Pray, brethren, that our sacrifice may be acceptable to God, the almighty Father.

People: May the Lord accept the sacrifice at your hands for the praise and glory of his name, for our good, and the good of all his Church.

Prayer Over the Gifts

At the end:

People: **Amen.**

EUCHARISTIC PRAYER

The priest offers the great Sacrifice.

Introductory dialogue

Priest: The Lord be with you.

People: And also with you.

Priest   Lift up your hearts.

People: We lift them up to the Lord.

Priest: Let us give thanks to the Lord our God.

People: It is right to give him thanks and praise.

Preface

Praise to the Father

Father, it is our duty and our
  salvation,
always and everywhere
to give you thanks
through your beloved Son, Jesus
  Christ.
He is the Word through whom
  you made the universe,
the Savior you sent to redeem us.
By the power of the Holy Spirit
he took flesh and was born of the
  Virgin Mary.
For our sake he opened his arms
  on the cross;
he put an end to death
and revealed the resurrection.
In this he fulfilled your will
and won for you a holy people.
And so we join the angels and
  the saints

in proclaiming your glory
as we sing (say):

Sanctus

First Acclamation of the People

Priest and people:

Holy, holy, holy Lord, God of
  power and might,
heaven and earth are full of
  your glory.
Hosanna in the highest.
Blessed is he who comes in the
  name of the Lord.
Hosanna in the highest.

Invocation of the Holy Spirit

Lord, you are holy indeed,
  the fountain of all holiness.
Let your Spirit come upon these
  gifts to make them holy,
so that they may become for us
the body and blood of our Lord,
  Jesus Christ.

The Lord's Supper

Before he was given up to death,
  a death he freely accepted,
he took bread and gave you thanks.
He broke the bread,
  gave it to his disciples, and said:

Take this, all of you, and eat it:
this is my body which will be
   given up for you.
When supper was ended, he took
   the cup.
Again he gave you thanks and praise,
gave the cup to his disciples,
   and said:
Take this, all of you, and drink
   from it:
this is the cup of my blood,
the blood of the new and everlasting
   covenant.
It will be shed for you and for all
so that sins may be forgiven.
Do this in memory of me.

Memorial Acclamation

Priest: Let us proclaim the mystery of faith:

People: Christ has died,
Christ is risen,
Christ will come again.

(or)

Dying you destroyed our death,
rising you restored our life,
Lord Jesus, come in glory.

(or)

When we eat this bread and
drink this cup,
we proclaim your death, Lord
Jesus,
until you come in glory.

(or)

Lord, by your cross and resurrection
You have set us free.
You are the Savior of the world.

In memory of his death and
   resurrection,
we offer you, Father, this
   life-giving bread,
   this saving cup.
We thank you for counting us
   worthy
to stand in your presence and
   serve you.

May all of us who share in the
   body and blood of Christ
be brought together in unity by
   the Holy Spirit.

Lord, remember your Church
  throughout the world;
make us grow in love,
together with N. our Pope,
N. our bishop, and all the clergy.

For the Dead

Remember our brothers and sisters
who have gone to their rest
in the hope of rising again;
bring them and all the departed
into the light of your presence.

In Communion with the Saints

Have mercy on us all;
make us worthy to share eternal
  life

with Mary, the virgin Mother of
   God,
   with the apostles,
and with all the saints who have
   done your will throughout the
   ages.

May we praise you in union
   with them,
and give you glory
through your Son, Jesus Christ.

Concluding Doxology

Through him,
with him,
in him,
in the unity of the Holy Spirit,
all glory and honor is yours,
almighty Father,
for ever and ever.

                    All reply: **Amen.**

39

COMMUNION RITE

The Lord's Prayer

Priest: Let us pray with confidence to the Father in the words our Savior gave us:

Priest and people: Our Father, who art in heaven, hallowed be thy name; thy kingdom come; thy will be done on earth as it is in heaven. Give us this day our daily bread; and forgive us our trespasses as we forgive those who trespass against us; and lead us not into temptation, but deliver us from evil.

Priest: **Deliver us, Lord, from every evil,**
and grant us peace in our day.
In your mercy keep us free from sin
and protect us from all anxiety
as we wait in joyful hope
for the coming of our Saviour,
Jesus Christ.

People: **For the kingdom, the power, and the glory are yours, now and for ever.**

Sign of Peace

(The priest says the prayer for peace and concludes: **for ever and ever.**)

People: **Amen.**

Priest: **The peace of the Lord be with you always.**

People: **And also with you.**

Deacon (or Priest):
Let us offer each other the sign of peace.

(The people exchange a sign of peace and love, according to local custom.)

Breaking of the Bread

(The people sing or say:)

Lamb of God, you take away the
    sins of the world:
  have mercy on us.
Lamb of God, you take away the
    sins of the world:
  have mercy on us.
Lamb of God, you take away the
    sins of the world:
  grant us peace.

*(Then the priest joins his hands and
says quietly:)*

Lord Jesus Christ, Son of the
    Living God,
by the will of the Father and the
    work of the Holy Spirit
your death brought life to the
    world.
By your holy body and blood
free me from all my sins and
    from every evil.

Keep me faithful to your teaching,
and never let me be parted from
you.

(or)

Lord Jesus Christ,
with faith in your love and mercy
I eat your body and drink your
blood.
Let it not bring me
condemnation,
but health in mind and body.

Communion

Priest: This is the Lamb of God
who takes away the sins of the
world.
        Happy are those who are
called to his supper.

Priest and people: Lord, I am not
worthy to receive you,
but only say the word and I shall
be healed.

Communion of the Priest

The priest says quietly:

**May the body of Christ bring
me to everlasting life.**

*He reverently consumes the body of
Christ.*

*The priest then takes the chalice and
says in a low voice:*

**May the blood of Christ bring
me to everlasting life.**

*He reverently drinks the blood of
Christ.*

Communion of the People

Priest: **The Body of Christ.**
Communicant: **Amen.**

After communion there may be a period of silence or a song of praise may be sung.

Prayer after Communion

Priest: **Let us pray.**

Everyone prays silently for a while.

Then the priest says the prayer after Communion. The people respond:

People: **Amen.**

CONCLUDING RITE

Now it is time for us to leave, to do good works, to praise and bless the Lord in our daily lives.
After any announcements, the blessing and dismissal follow.

Blessing

Priest: **The Lord be with you.**
People: **And also with you.**

Priest: **May almighty God bless you, the Father, and the Son, ✝ and the Holy Spirit.**
People: **Amen.**

Dismissal

Deacon (or Priest):

Go in the peace of Christ:

(or)

The Mass is ended, go in peace.

(or)

Go in peace to love and serve the Lord.

People: **Thanks be to God.**

51

THE CHURCH YEAR

The seasons of the Church year are: Advent, Christmas, Lent, Easter, Pentecost and Ordinary Time.

Advent means coming. Each year for four weeks before Christmas, Christians prepare their minds and hearts for the birth of Jesus.

The six weeks before Easter are called Lent. For Christians, Lent is a time of special prayer, reflection and self-denial. The first Easter was the day Jesus fulfilled his promise and arose from the dead.

Pentecost celebrates the day the disciples were gathered together and the Holy Spirit entered them. The spirit gave them the courage to be like Jesus.

During the remaining weeks, a season called Ordinary Time, the church invites us to learn more about Jesus and his Spirit in us.

One cold, quiet night long ago, a man named Joseph travelled with his wife, Mary, across the desert to a small town called Bethlehem.

When they arrived in Bethlehem they searched everywhere trying to find a place where they might rest for the night. Finding no inn, they took shelter in a small stable.

There, among the sheep, oxen, and straw, Mary gave birth to a son and she named Him Jesus. Angels rejoiced and the world fell sweetly silent, wrapped in a wonderous peace, for Jesus, the infant born in the stable, was the Son of God. The King and Savior of the universe had come to live among men.

It came to pass that a star appeared in the heavens. Its beautiful bright light fell upon shepherds tending their flocks in the fields. It

fell upon three wisemen, each a king of a country, as they, too, travelled across the desert. An Angel of the Lord appeared to the shepherds and to the wisemen, telling them to follow the star so that they might see the newborn King.

When the Wisemen saw Jesus they knew at once that He was not just the King of a country, but the King of all men everywhere. They knew He was the King of Kings sent by God to save all men. They honored Him with gifts of Gold, Frankincense, and Myrrh.

News of Jesus' birth spread far and near. People everywhere shared the good news that a new King had been born! A King who would be the Savior of all men!

This news made King Herod very upset. King Herod thought that he should be the only King of whom

people spoke. He sent his servants out to find the Baby Jesus.

But God's ever loving and knowing ways saved Jesus. God sent one of His angels to tell Joseph to take Mary and Jesus to a land called Egypt where they would be safe.

After some time had passed Joseph and Mary returned to their home with their son. They took Him to the Temple to present Him to God, as this was the custom of their people. At the Temple they offered two doves in thanksgiving for His birth, and they named Him Jesus.

In the Temple was a very old man named Simeon. He had long prayed to God to let him live long enough to see the coming of God's Son. As he held the infant in his hands he knew his prayer had been answered. As soon as he looked upon Jesus he proclaimed to all that Jesus was the

"Savior of the World." Anna, an elderly woman of the Temple, saw Jesus and began to tell everyone that the Savior had come.

Jesus grew up in a tiny village called Nazareth. He spent His days playing with His friends and working by His father's side learning the trade of carpentry.

Joseph taught Jesus how to shape the wood into many beautiful things. Together they made chairs, tables, furniture and toys. Jesus learned well. Many people called Him the carpenter's son.

Mary and Joseph also taught their Son how to study and think about God's Holy Word. Jesus learned quickly. He was a joy to His parents' heart for He was loving, kind, and obedient.

Once, when Jesus was twelve, He went with His parents to Jerusalem

to celebrate a holiday. When the celebration had ended, all the travellers packed their things and began the journey back to Nazareth. At this time Mary thought that Jesus was travelling with Joseph, and Joseph thought that Jesus was travelling with Mary!

When night time came Mary and Joseph realized that Jesus was not with them. They searched all through their group, but, could not find their son. Not knowing what to do, they began walking back to Jerusalem. It was a day later when they found Jesus. He was standing on the steps of the Temple speaking to the elders about God's Word. All who heard Him were amazed at His wisdom.

Jesus had a cousin named John who was a man of God, too. John travelled the countryside calling to the people to repent of their sins and turn back to God.

God's power was in John's words. Many people thought John was the Savior. But John told the people that he had only come to prepare the way for the true Savior.

One day Jesus came to the river to be baptised by John. It was then that John heard the voice of the Lord say, "This is My beloved Son, whom I love. Follow Him."

Many people came from great distances to hear Jesus preach God's Word. They asked Him to teach them how to pray. That's when Jesus gave us the Lord's prayer. He told us that the best way to show our love for Him is to keep His commandments.

Of all the many people who followed Jesus, He chose 12 men to be His Apostles. The Apostles travelled everywhere with Jesus. He taught them many things about God's way. He gave to them the task of spreading God's word to all the nations of the world.

News of Jesus' teachings continued to spread throughout the land. In one of the places Jesus visited 5,000 people sat on a hillside for 5 hours in the hot sun just so they could hear the words of the Lord.

Jesus was touched by their devotion. He knew that many of them had travelled a great distance to hear Him, and now they would have to travel home without food or water. He asked His Apostles to find some food so that He might feed His followers.

All that the Apostles could find was a boy who had five loaves of bread and two fish. Jesus prayed to His heavenly Father and told the Apostles to pass out the loaves and fish. To their surprise there was enough to feed the 5,000 people all they wanted. When the meal was finished, the Apostles gathered twelve baskets of scraps! It was a miracle. A miracle brought about by Jesus' love.

Jesus performed many miracles. He made the blind see, the crippled walk, He made the deaf hear, and even brought some people back to life. He would perform these miracles with only the slightest touch of His hand or a word He spoke. His love was so great He had the power to cure men of anything that ailed them.

Always, when Jesus performed a miracle, He let the people know that the miracle came from the power of God. He told the people that He performed miracles so that people might come to understand His Father's love for them, and give glory to God's name.

The people loved Jesus so much! Wherever He travelled they brought their sick for Him to cure. They brought their children for Him to hold. Jesus loved the little children. He always had His Apostles bring the little children to Him.

He once told all the other people that they must become child like to enter fully into God's kingdom. Jesus called on the people to remember that all peoples everywhere are children of God. He asked that we live in peace together.

Not everyone was happy to know that God had sent Jesus to the world to save us from our sins. There was a group of people who plotted against Jesus. They wanted people to follow their word, not Jesus. They had Jesus arrested for false reasons because they did not believe that Jesus was the Son of God.

Jesus' Apostles and followers became angry and frightened. They did not know what to do. Jesus told them not to worry because everything was happening according to God's plan.

That is how Jesus came to die for our sins. He obeyed His Father's commandments so much that He gave His life so that we could be saved from our sins. Before He was taken to His cross, Jesus told His followers that He would rise again in three days. They were not sure what Jesus' words meant. They did not know what to think. They only knew that Jesus was being taken to die on the hill of Calvary.

That afternoon, hanging on the cross with two thieves beside Him, Jesus showed the perfection of His love. In the midst of all His pain and agony, He asked His Father to forgive the people who had crucified

Him. He told God that they had not known what they had done. Having asked this, Jesus hung His head and sent His spirit back to God.

Three days later when His Apostles went to visit Jesus' tomb, they found it was empty! Jesus had risen from the dead, just as He proclaimed He would!

Of all the lessons Jesus taught to people in His life, the greatest lesson came when He came back to life. Jesus showed us that God's love has power over all things, even death! He taught us and He showed us that those who love God will have life with Him forever!

And He showed us that the best way to show our love for God is to keep His commandments. If we do this, we will be sure to live with Jesus forever!

PRAYERS
AND
DEVOTIONS

RECONCILIATION

Jesus has asked us to love God with all our heart, all our mind and all our soul; and to love our neighbor as ourself.

Sometimes we do not follow Jesus and we fail to love as we should. This separates us from God. It is the way we sin.

But Jesus loves us too much to let us remain apart. He wants very much to forgive us if only we go to him, say we are sorry and promise to do better. This we do through the Sacrament of Reconciliation.

EXAMINATION
OF CONSCIENCE

Before confessing your sins, it is important to look at your life and ask yourself some questions:

Have I behaved as God's child should?

Do I pray to God every day?

Have I given trouble to my parents and teachers?

Have I been selfish in my dealings with others?

Have I been honest and truthful?

Have I quarreled and not tried to make friends again?

Have I neglected my work in school or at home?

Do I respect my body and take good care of it?

Do I help those who are poor or handicapped or have other needs?

Do I show the old, the sick or the lonely that I care about them?

When going to confession, either in the Reconciliation Room or behind the confessional screen, always remember that the priest represents Jesus. There is no need to be afraid. The priest is there to help you. He will show you how to let Jesus come into your life.

RECEIVING THE SACRAMENT

After you greet the priest, make the Sign of the Cross. The priest will bless you and may read a passage from Holy Scripture. If he does, listen carefully to God's Word.

You then will speak to the priest about your sins. Tell him whatever is keeping you away from God and preventing you from being a better follower of Jesus.

When you are finished, the priest will counsel you and may ask you to say a prayer or do something to show your sorrow. He may ask you to recite an Act of Contrition. Then the priest will say the words of absolution and reconciliation.

When you leave, remember to thank the priest. Then remain a few moments in church and tell Jesus how happy and grateful you are because your sins are forgiven.

THE STATIONS
OF THE CROSS

Each Good Friday we recall the passion of Jesus, the day he suffered and died on the cross.

On the first Good Friday, almost 2000 years ago, Jesus made many stops on the way to Calvary. The fourteen pictures around the walls of our church remind us of all that happened on that sad day.

A good way to thank Jesus is to visit each station, think of what happened and tell Jesus how much we love him.

First Station
JESUS MEETS PILATE

Jesus' first stop on the way of the cross is the Governor's palace. Many Jewish leaders want Jesus out of the way. "Crucify him," they insist. And they influence Pilate the Governor to condemn Jesus to death.

Second Station
JESUS TAKES THE CROSS

The Roman Soldiers bring a large wooden cross for Jesus to carry. It is very heavy and rough. Though Jesus is tired, sick, and weak, he reaches out and accepts the cross lovingly. By his love he transforms this cross into a symbol of hope and salvation for all people.

Third Station

JESUS FALLS

Soon after he begins to carry the cross, Jesus falls. He is very exhausted and the weight of the cross crushes him. The soldiers roughly drag him to his feet and Jesus slowly continues his painful journey.

Fourth Station

JESUS MEETS HIS MOTHER

On the narrow roadway, Jesus turns the corner and looks ahead to see his mother. She reaches out to touch him. He is thankful that she is there. She doesn't say anything to him, but he knows that she loves him even though she feels sad and helpless to do anything.

Fifth Station
SIMON HELPS JESUS

The soldiers notice that Jesus is very weak. He is staggering under the load, so they pull a man from the crowd—a stranger—and force him to help Jesus carry his cross. The stranger, whose name is Simon Cyrene, is frightened and doesn't know who Jesus is.

Sixth Station
VERONICA WIPES JESUS' FACE

A woman named Veronica steps out from the crowd with a towel. Jesus' hands are holding his cross, so she wipes his face, which is dripping with blood and sweat. Veronica does a simple act of kindness to show she cares.

Seventh Station
JESUS FALLS AGAIN

The soldiers let Simon go his way and Jesus is again carrying the cross by himself. There is still a long way to go. Jesus staggers and falls. He is breathing very heavily and has no strength left. Yet he stands up. And because of his strong love, he is able to go forward.

Eighth Station
JESUS MEETS SOME WOMEN

Jesus meets a group of women from Jerusalem. They are weeping because he is suffering so much. Jesus tells them to weep for themselves and for their children, because the cruelty in the world will surely touch them just as it is touching him.

Ninth Station

JESUS FALLS A THIRD TIME

A third time Jesus falls. He has no more strength left. He has lost much blood and the hot sun burns his skin. Again he struggles to stand up because he has chosen the way of the cross out of love for us.

Tenth Station

JESUS IS STRIPPED

Jesus has reached the top of the hill. The soldiers let him drop the cross to the ground. And while Jesus stands there in front of the crowds, the soldiers pull off his clothes leaving him embarrassed and humiliated. He is being treated as a common criminal, as if he were a worthless human being.

Eleventh Station
JESUS IS NAILED TO THE CROSS

Now the soldiers make Jesus lie down on the cross. They stretch out his arms and fasten them with nails. They also nail his feet so that he is securely fastened to the cross. He cannot escape. Only his great love for us enables Jesus to bear his pain and suffering.

Twelfth Station
JESUS DIES

The cross is standing and Jesus is hanging on it. Time goes by very slowly, for Jesus is full of pain. But more important than the pain is his love for us and his willingness to die for us to be free from sin.

Thirteenth Station
JESUS IS PLACED IN MARY'S ARMS

After Jesus dies, a few friends gently take his body down from the cross and put it in the arms of his mother. She held Jesus like this when he was a baby, but now his body has no life left in it. Her heart is filled with sadness.

Fourteenth Station
JESUS IS BURIED

The final stopping place for Jesus on this sad day is a tomb. His friends place his body on the stone slab, wipe off the blood, wash his body clean, and cover it with cloth and nice-smelling spices. His friends and mother touch his body for the last time before they leave.

After we recall the Fourteen Stations, it is good to remember what follows Good Friday. Jesus' story does not end in sadness but in joy. He not only died, but on Easter Sunday he rose out of his tomb gloriously alive.

Jesus' Father, who is God, willed to allow Jesus to die out of love for us. He also willed to bring Jesus back to life so that in Jesus we would have no fear of death. Jesus will lead us through death to new life.

THE ROSARY

The rosary is a special way of praying to God that honors Mary, the Mother of Jesus. While reciting prayers, you think about certain stories in the lives of Jesus and Mary. These stories are called mysteries: a mystery is a story about God.

Rosary beads are used to keep count of the prayers and mysteries. Recite the Apostles' Creed while you hold the crucifix, then one Our Father and three Hail Marys. After that, as you think about each mystery, recite the Our Father on the large bead, the Hail Mary on each of ten smaller beads and finish with a Glory Be. That makes one decade. The complete rosary consists of five decades. There are three sets of mysteries and five stories in each set.

THE JOYFUL MYSTERIES

1. The Coming of Jesus is Announced
2. Mary Visits Elizabeth
3. Jesus is Born
4. Jesus is Presented to God
5. Jesus is Found in the Temple

THE SORROWFUL MYSTERIES

1. Jesus' Agony in the Garden
2. Jesus is Whipped
3. Jesus is Crowned with Thorns
4. Jesus Carries His Cross
5. Jesus Dies on the Cross

THE GLORIOUS MYSTERIES

1. Jesus Rises from His Tomb
2. Jesus Ascends to Heaven
3. The Holy Spirit Descends
4. Mary is Assumed into Heaven
5. Mary is Crowned in Heaven

THE SACRAMENTS

Christ instituted seven sacraments. They are outward visible signs of God's grace given at special moments in a person's life. They help us live our lives more fully.

BAPTISM

Baptism is also called christening. It is the first sacrament we receive, and makes us members of the church. It is performed by pouring water on a person's forehead, and saying "I baptize you in the name of the Father, and of the Son, and of the Holy Spirit. Amen."

CONFIRMATION

Confirmation bestows the special seal or mark of the Holy Spirit. It gives you the special spiritual energy to make Jesus known in the world, and the courage to live the way Jesus would like you to live.

HOLY EUCHARIST

Communion is often called the greatest sacrament because Christ himself is present in the consecrated bread and wine. The bread and wine are transformed into Christ's body and blood by the priest during mass.

RECONCILIATION

This sacrament brings us God's forgiveness through the words of a priest. Reconciliation makes us holy and reconciles us with God and the Church. This used to be called "Penance" or "Confession."

ANOINTING OF THE SICK

This sacrament is for the seriously ill, the infirm and the very old. The sacrament of the sick sanctifies sufferings, increases grace, forgives sins and makes us ready for heaven.

HOLY ORDERS

This sacrament gives priests the power to forgive sins, the power to anoint the sick, the power to change bread and wine into the body and blood of Christ, and the power to perpetuate Jesus' sacrifice, which is the Mass. Through Holy Orders, priests and bishops receive the Spirit's grace to guide the church and take care of the people of God.

MATRIMONY

This sacrament is received when a husband and wife pronounce their marriage vows. It gives the grace for two people to join their lives together until death. The husband and wife perform this sacrament for each other. The priest is only the official church witness of this sacrament. Matrimony also enables people to be good mothers and fathers.

THE TEN COMMANDMENTS

1. I am the Lord your God. You shall not have strange gods before me.
2. You shall not take the Name of the Lord your God in vain.
3. Remember to keep holy the Lord's Day.
4. Honor your father and your mother.
5. You shall not kill.
6. You shall not commit adultery.
7. You shall not steal.
8. You shall not bear false witness against your neighbor.
9. You shall not covet your neighbor's wife.
10. You shall not covet your neighbor's goods.

THE PRECEPTS
OF THE CHURCH

1. To attend Mass every Sunday and holy day of obligation.
2. To celebrate the Sacrament of Reconciliation at least once a year; and to receive Holy Communion during Easter time.
3. To study Catholic teaching in preparation for the Sacrament of Confirmation and then to continue our religious education.
4. To observe the marriage laws of the Church.
5. To strengthen and support the Church.
6. To do penance, including abstaining and fasting on the appointed days.
7. To join in the missionary spirit and apostolate of the Church.

THE BEATITUDES

1. Blessed are the poor in spirit, for the kingdom of heaven is theirs.

2. Blessed are those who are sad, for they shall be comforted.

3. Blessed are the mild and gentle, for they shall inherit the land.

4. Blessed are those who hunger and thirst for justice, for they shall be filled.

5. Blessed are the merciful, for they shall receive mercy.

6. Blessed are the pure in heart, for they shall see God.

7. Blessed are those who make peace, for they shall be called the children of God.

8. Blessed are those who suffer for my sake, for heaven will be theirs.

THE CHIEF SPIRITUAL WORKS OF MERCY

To admonish the sinner.
To instruct the ignorant.
To counsel the doubtful.
To comfort the sorrowful.
To bear wrongs patiently.
To forgive all injuries.
To pray for the living and the dead.

THE CHIEF CORPORAL WORKS OF MERCY

To feed the hungry.
To give drink to the thirsty.
To clothe the naked.
To visit the imprisoned.
To shelter the homeless.
To visit the sick.
To bury the dead.

MEMORY PRAYERS

To pray is to talk to God or to think about Him. Sometimes we pray in our own words and tell what is deep in our hearts. Other times we say the prayers known by all Catholics. Some of these prayers are listed below. You should memorize them so you can say them at any time of the day or night.

THE SIGN OF THE CROSS

In the name of the Father
and of the Son ✝
and of the Holy Spirit.
Amen.

THE OUR FATHER

Our Father, who art in heaven, hallowed be thy name; thy kingdom come; thy will be done on earth as it is in heaven. Give us this day our daily bread; and forgive us our trespasses as we forgive those who trespass against us and lead us not into temptation, but deliver us from evil. Amen.

THE HAIL MARY

Hail Mary, full of grace, The Lord is with thee. Blessed art thou amongst women, and blessed is the fruit of thy womb, Jesus. Holy Mary, Mother of God, pray for us sinners, now and at the hour of our death. Amen.

THE GLORY BE

Glory be to the Father, and to the Son, and to the Holy Spirit, as it was in the beginning, is now, and ever shall be, world without end. Amen.

THE APOSTLES' CREED

I believe in God, the Father almighty creator of heaven and earth. I believe in Jesus Christ, his only Son, our Lord. He was conceived by the power of the Holy Spirit and born of the Virgin Mary. He suffered under Pontius Pilate, was crucified, died, and was buried. He decended to the dead. On the third day he rose again. He ascended into heaven, and is seated at the right hand of the Father. He will come again to judge the living and the dead. I believe in the Holy Spirit, the holy catholic Church, the communion of saints, the forgiveness of sins, the resurrection of the body, and the life everlasting. Amen.

ACT OF CONTRITION

O my God, I am heartily sorry for having offended you and I detest all my sins, because of your punishments, but most of all because they offend you, my God, who are all-good and deserving of all my love. I firmly resolve, with the help of your grace, to sin no more and to avoid the near occasions of sin. Amen.

GRACE BEFORE MEALS

Bless us, O Lord, and these your gifts, which we are about to receive from your goodness, through Christ our Lord. Amen.

GRACE AFTER MEALS

We thank you, O Lord, for these gifts and for all the gifts we have received from your goodness, through Christ our Lord. Amen.

THE "MEMORARE"

Remember, O most gracious Virgin Mary, that never was it known that anyone who fled to your protection, implored your help or sought your intercession, was left unaided. Inspired with this confidence, I fly to

you, O Virgin of virgins, my Mother; to you do I come, before you I stand, sinful and sorrowful. O Mother of the Word Incarnate, despise not my petitions, but in your mercy hear and answer me. Amen.

PRAYER TO THE HOLY SPIRIT

Come, O Holy Spirit, fill the hearts of Your faithful and kindle in them the fire of Your love.

V.Send forth Your Spirit
    and they shall be created
R.And You shall renew
    the face of the earth.

Let us pray:
O God, who has taught the hearts of the faithful by the light of the Holy Spirit, grant that in the same Spirit, we may be always truly wise and ever rejoice in His consolation. Through Christ our Lord. Amen.

MORNING PRAYER

Dear God, I thank you for watching over me during the night. Today I offer you my whole self: my every thought, word and act. Please keep me from harm. Bless my parents, my family and everyone I love.

EVENING PRAYER

Dear God, before I go to bed, please hear my last prayer. Thank you for all your help today. Forgive me for any wrong I did. I am truly sorry. Keep in your care, my mother and father, and everyone I love. May the souls of the faithful departed, through the mercy of God, rest in peace. Amen.

A VISIT TO CHURCH

It is most pleasing to God when we make a visit to Church and speak to Jesus quietly and alone.

If we do this often, we shall grow very close to our Lord and his grace will be with us to guide our every moment.

In addition to our own words and thoughts, the following prayers may be said:

ACT OF FAITH

O my God, I believe that you are one God in three Divine Persons: Father, Son and Holy Spirit. I believe that Your Divine Son became Man and died for our sins, and that He will come again to judge the living and the dead. I believe these and all the truths that the Catholic Church teaches, because You have revealed them, who can neither deceive nor be deceived. Amen.

ACT OF HOPE

O my God, relying on Your almighty power and infinite mercy and promises, I hope to obtain pardon of my sins, the help of Your grace and life everlasting through the merits of Jesus Christ, my Lord and Redeemer. Amen.

ACT OF LOVE

O my God, I love you above all things with my whole heart and soul, because You are all good and worthy of all my love. I love my neighbor as myself for the love of You. I forgive all who have injured me and ask pardon of all whom I have injured. Amen.

PRAYER BEFORE A CRUCIFIX

Look down upon me, good and gentle Jesus, while I kneel and ask you to fill my heart with faith, hope, charity and true sorrow for my sins. Help me never to sin again.

I think of your five wounds with great love and pity as I repeat the words of your prophet, David, "They have pierced my hands and my feet; they have injured all my bones."

(Say one Our Father, Hail Mary, and Glory be, for the Pope)

PERSONAL RECORD

Name _____

   born _____ in _____

Baptism

  Date _____

  Priest _____

  Parish _____

  Godfather _____

  Godmother _____

First Communion

  Date _____

  Priest _____

  Parish _____

Confirmation

  Date _____

  Bishop _____

  Parish _____

  Sponsor _____

  Confirmation name _____

FAMILY RECORD

Father _____

    born _____ in _____

Mother _____

    born _____ in _____

Father's family

    Grandfather _____

        born _____

    Grandmother _____

        born _____

Mother's family _____

    Grandfather _____

        born _____

    Grandmother _____

        born _____